AF574800

Other Books by G. Michael Dobbs

Escape.
How Animation Broke into the Mainstream in the 1990's.

15 Minutes With...
Forty Years of Interviews

Springfield.
Postcard History of Springfield, Massachusetts

Tales from the Runway.
Written as Bill Brazil with at by Danielle Holmes

Made of Pen & Ink:
Fleischer Studios, The New York years

Made of Pen & Ink:
Fleischer Studios, The Florida years

What They Didn't Teach You In Journalism School

The Memoir Of An Ink-Stained Wretch

G. Michael DOBBS

inkwell productions TM

Published by
Inkwell Productions
Office of Publication:
17 Spruce Street
Springfield, MA 01105 USA

In association with
Not Dog Books

First Edition: May 2024
ISBN 978-1-7330144-7-2

What They Didn't Teach You In Journalism School:
The Memoir Of An Ink-Stained Wretch.

For more information or comments, e-mail us at gmdobbs@comcast.net

Dedication

First, this modest book is fondly dedicated to all of us ink-stained wretches,

Those of us who consider two doughnuts and a coffee a breakfast,

Those who have learned the art of waiting for a politician to turn up at a press conference – always late,

Those who have developed a bad habit or two,

Those who pride themselves on their cynicism,

Those who can tell you which gas station has the best hot dog,

Those who have gritted their teeth while their editor or publisher was talking crap,

Those who debate if an interview subject is worth wearing a tie,

Those who realize public relations people make more money than they do,

Those who, despite what they have seen are still, in their heart of hearts, advocates for democracy, And those who endure civic meetings filled with theatrics and bluster that run for hours.

Second, I must add that all of us who have partners or spouses should be thankful for their support for a job with odd hours, relatively low pay and way too much angst.

Lastly, I want to recognize an honorary ink-stained wretch (in many ways he is indeed one), my friend Anthony Cignoli.

Introduction

I was very uneasy with writing any memoir of sorts as that kind of thing is usually reserved for the famous or infamous, of which I am neither.

My friend Joseph Citro of Vermont made the case that I should try this interesting format of writing 100 chapters each 100 words long. Now Joe is the author of many books, some non-fiction horror and some like "Weird New England," that collects folklore as well as the odd side of New England history. He is in much demand as a speaker in the Green Mountain State where he has been given the title "The Bard of Bizarre."

By the way, I heartily recommend Joe's book "Loose Change," which inspired this book.

Unlike Joe, I'm a simply an old working journalist, still in the saddle despite retirement, who has achieved some recognition in one small part of the world. What I wanted to do with this effort was to offer a look at the path I took and what I learned from that journey that was not covered in journalism program at the University of Massachusetts circa 1972-1976.

I do this in the hopes I could offer younger journalists some ground-level advice if they chose to accept it.

There is frequently a feeling that with the incredible changes in technology of the past 30 years that people like me are truly relics of the past. The changes have made the job much easier than it once was, but the fundamentals of interviewing, building relationships, as well as other details of being a reporter have remained the same.

The observations I offer are those from small to medium media markets. Working in such a market has not prevented me from interviewing celebrities, governors, senators and members of Congress and I hope this book underscores the importance of taking advantage of every situation for a story.

For example, when I was on talk radio, I learned the first lady of the American film industry, Lillian Gish, was reissuing her autobiography. I thought this would be a great segment for my program and as a movie fan I was thrilled at the prospect of speaking to someone of her historical status. The publicist at her publisher squashed the idea but I decided I wouldn't let it go. I looked up her agent and asked her if Gish would be interested in an interview. She was and the conversation was excellent. I subsequently sold it as a story to a local newspaper.

So, my first bit of advice is to not accept that "no" so readily. Seek a work around to get your story.

I refer to myself as an "ink-stained wretch" in the title of this book. One of the mayors I covered, Michael Bissonnette of Chicopee, MA, called me that quite frequently. I found this definition online, "The phrase 'ink-stained wretch' typically refers to a journalist or writer, emphasizing the idea of someone who works hard and is dedicated to their craft. The term 'ink-stained' refers to the traditional use of ink in writing and printing, while 'wretch' can convey a sense of toil or struggle. The phrase is often used to romanticize the hard work and dedication of those in the writing profession. There isn't a specific story associated with the phrase, but it has been used in literature and journalism to describe individuals who labor in the pursuit of truth and storytelling."

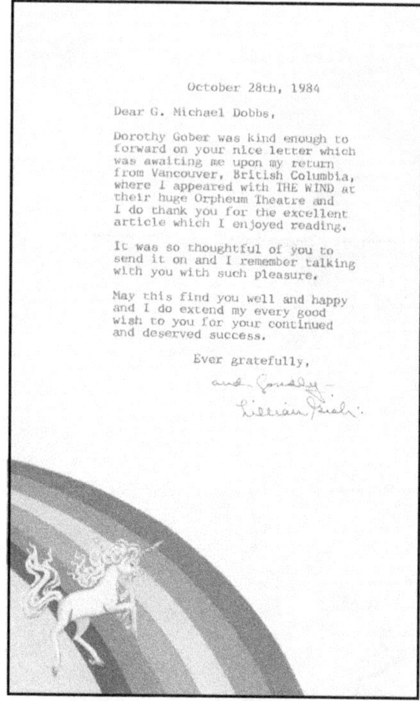

October 28th, 1984

Dear G. Michael Dobbs,

Dorothy Gober was kind enough to forward on your nice letter which was awaiting me upon my return from Vancouver, British Columbia, where I appeared with THE WIND at their huge Orpheum Theatre and I do thank you for the excellent article which I enjoyed reading.

It was so thoughtful of you to send it on and I remember talking with you with such pleasure.

May this find you well and happy and I do extend my every good wish to you for your continued and deserved success.

Ever gratefully,

and fondly —

Lillian Gish.

Lillian Gish sent me a very nice note after our interview.

And considering I frequently use a fountain pen, I am indeed ink-stained.

I hope dear reader you will get something out of this exercise. I certainly enjoyed writing it. I would love to hear your reactions at gmdobbs@comcast.net, if they are positive, if not, well I'm retired, so I say with fondness, go to hell.

G. Michael Dobbs - 2024

The boys meeting at Smokey Joe's Cigar Lounge in Springfield, MA. From left to right, the ink-stained wretch; illustrator, author and book designer Mark Masztal; the man who inspired this book, Joe Citro; and cartoonist and film historian Stephen R. Bissette.

Table of Contents

Why Did You Become A Writer . 1
Me... 2
Unrelentingly Working Class...... 3
Earliest Memory......................... 4
Springfield................................. 5
My First Brush With celebrity 6
Moving...................................... 7
Movies...................................... 8
The Movie 9
Florida...................................... 10
Illinois 11
Hadley....................................... 12
Another Movie 13
Okinawa................................... 14
Bomb Scare 15
Another move........................... 16
Farm Life Is For Me.................. 17
Inertron.................................... 18
Freak Show............................... 19
High School 20
First Controversey 21
The Transcript-Telegram........... 22
Composition 23
Celebrities 24
Freelancing Starts...................... 25
In Person 26
Gaines Once More 27
Thou Shall Not Waste............... 28
The Hubris Of Youth................ 29
After College 30
Freelancing............................... 31
Life Changes............................. 32
First Gig 33
Westfield Evening News 34
Back To The T-T....................... 35
Have a Backup Plan.................. 36
Talk Radio................................ 37
Interviews................................. 38
Who Did I Talk With?............. 39
Commercials 40
The Freakiest Moment.............. 41
Side Hustle............................... 42
Leaving Radio........................... 43
Skin Of My Teeth...................... 44
Tower Theaters 45
Comics..................................... 46
My MBA.................................. 47
Gun To My Head..................... 48
Animato 49
Animato Part 2......................... 50
Animato Part 3......................... 51
All Good Things End................ 52
Lessons In Public Relations....... 53
Lessons In Public Relations 2.... 54
Lessons In Public Relations 3.... 54
Goodbye................................... 56

Table of Contents cont.

Back To Journalism.................. 57
Print Is Not Dead.................... 58
Wonderful People.................... 59
Democracy.............................. 60
Television 61
Retirement 62
Books 63
Geezer 64
Role Models 65
The Practical Advice I Received 66
Your Publishers May Understand Nothing.................................. 67
Mentors.................................. 68
Know Your Civics.................... 69
Agendas Are Your Friends......... 70
Go With The Flow 71
In-Person Or Remote 72
Relationships.......................... 73
Colleagues 74
Editors.................................... 75
Editors Part 2 76
Editors Part 3 77
Editors Part 4 78
They Are Not Your Friend 79
People Only Tell You What They Want You To Know 80
Be Sure You Make Clear What Is On And Off The Record.......... 81
They Leave It Up To You 82
People Will Lie........................ 83
You Kids Today 84
Interviewing Part 1: Understand The Contract.......................... 85
Interviewing Part 2: Do Your Research................................. 86
Interviewing Part 3: Icebreakers 87
Interviewing Part 4: Try Not To Repeat Questions Already Asked 88
Interviewing Part 5: Know Your Time....................................... 89
Interviewing Part 6: Listen........ 90
Interviewing Part 7: Sometimes They Are Assholes.................... 91
Reviews Are Fun But Make Them Worthwhile 92
Look At The Damn Weather Forecast But Don't Trust It........ 93
Wear Sensible Shoes 94
Figure Out Your Own System For Taking Notes.......................... 95
Where Do I Go On Election Night? 96
Someone Wants you To Eat An Assignment............................. 97
Public Relations People Can Be Your Friend 98
Selfies 99
Have A Good Time 100

Chapter 1

WHO THE HELL AM I AND HOW DID I GET HERE?

Note: The names have been omitted of the people who made my life hellish but send me a dollar and I'll tell you who they are.

WHY DID YOU BECOME A WRITER? My dad, an avid reader, once asked me that question during my college years. He and my mom wanted me to be a high school teacher. They were afraid of the financial instability of being a writer, especially a journalist. They were right in that if you're looking to earn a lot of money, being a newspaper reporter or editor is not the way to achieve that goal. I never answered my father because I didn't know what to say. Today I know that I really had no choice. I yam what I yam.

Chapter 2

ME. Born in 1954 in Roswell, NM. My dad, Gordon, was in the Air Force and then later a teacher, and my mom Sue was a homemaker. I have one brother, Patrick. I attended eight different school districts in my first eight years of school. After my dad retired, we settled in Granby, MA. High school graduation was in 1972 and college (University of Massachusetts) was in 1976. I married my wife Mary in 1978. We have one foster daughter, three grandchildren and have had many pets, right now feeding three indoor cats, one feral cat and a handsome possum.

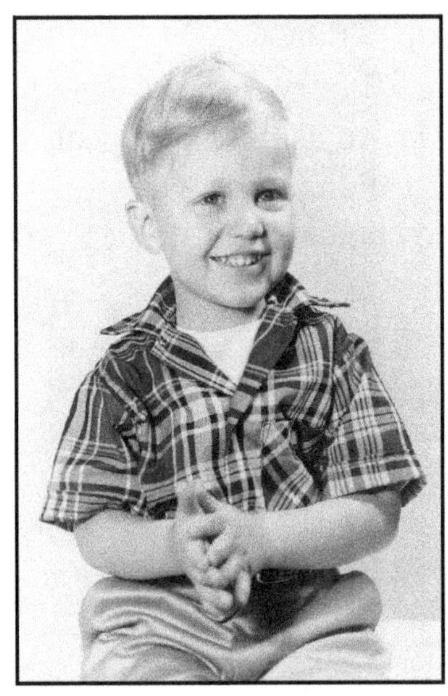

The author as a beardless youth.

Chapter 3

UNRELENTINGLY WORKING CLASS. There was no pretense in my family. My mom came from modest means in California and my dad was raised in poverty in Alabama. The Depression shaped them both, especially my dad. They both worked very hard. My parents, though, put much stock in education. Reading was a huge activity in my house as was going to museums, both art and historical. Learning a musical instrument was deemed very important. After dad's retirement from the Air Force, we had a small farm, which furthered my practical education. I take pride in knowing how to pluck a chicken.

My family: brother Patrick, our Grandmother Edith Gage, our mom and dad.

Chapter 4

EARLIEST MEMORY. I'm standing in the living room of 104 Navajo Road in Springfield, MA. I'm three years old. We had moved to Springfield in 1957, shortly after the birth of my brother. My dad had been assigned to Westover Air Force Base where he commanded and piloted a B-52 bomber carrying a nuclear payload. The sun is pouring into the room through the large front window and my little shadow is cast against the other wall where there is a sofa with a Native American-designed blanket on it. In my mind this image is like a still color photo.

Chapter 5

SPRINGFIELD. For years I told people I was from Springfield even though I wasn't born there and had lived in many other places. The answer to where I was from was complicated and I always considered Springfield home. One day a few years ago, I saw a friend whose father had been mayor, a man I respected and liked. I asked about his dad and my friend said, "Do you know why my dad likes you so much? You're a Springfield guy." I came home to my wife and said that Charlie Ryan had baptized me. I was very happy.

Welcome to Springfield!

Chapter 6

MY FIRST BRUSH WITH CELEBRITY. In 1960, my mom made an appointment to bring my brother and I to see the celebrated children's author Thornton W. Burgess, who lived nearby. A Burgess book was the first I checked out of the library and I loved his stories. The experience had a very profound effect on me. Burgess was extremely gracious and showed us around his writing studio. We bought several autographed books and I went home wrapping my six-year-old head around the idea that I had met an author. Is this why I wanted to be a writer years later?

This autographed book remains a prized part of my collection.

Chapter 7

MOVING. Living around the country as an Air Force kid was an adventure. I don't recall ever being upset that we were moving again. Dad would come home and make the announcement and away we would go. I enjoyed some places more than others. Montgomery, AL, was like living in a foreign country. I was told I talked funny. I talked funny? There were kids in my third-grade class who were barefoot daily. We sang "Dixie" every morning after pledging allegiance. The principal used a large wooden paddle for punishing kids. The cafeteria served hot dogs that were dyed red.

Chapter 8

MOVIES. In Montgomery I had a short-lived habit of going to the movies. Our parents would drop my brother and me off to a theater for a kiddie matinee. I loved it until the day we walked in the theater at the end of the feature and I saw a huge brain with a lone eyeball on the screen. I freaked out and dragged my younger brother out of the theater. I tried calling my parents to pick us up but they weren't home. We stood outside for two hours and I was in deep trouble for a long time.

Chapter 9

THE MOVIE. Because of its impact on my young life, I should note the film was "Journey to the Seventh Planet," an American-Danish co-production starring John Agar and made in 1962. The brain was an alien that could take over the minds of the American astronauts exploring Uranus. It could project their worst fears or greatest desires. Many, many years later my buddy Steve Bissette bought me a copy on DVD. I was clearly a very easy to frighten youth. It is a low-budget cheesy film at best and the brain monster is not impressive or frightening to adult standards.

The movie. I was an idiot kid because this stupid monster scared me out of the theater.

Chapter 10

FLORIDA. One day in Springfield, my dad, tired of the winters, bought property in Florida sight unseen. When in Montgomery, we took a trip south to see the property. It was a glorious trip, our only family vacation. We stayed in a state park with racoons, wild boars and alligators. Along the way we saw other developments that were clearly swamp land. Thankfully, mom's and dad's property was high and dry and they talked about building here when he retired. That never happened though and they sold the property holding the note for the buyers. They lost their complete investment.

Chapter 11

ILLINOIS. My dad went to a school at Chanute AFB in Rantoul, IL, next. The base had a collection of vintage aircraft which always impressed me. We lived on base and there was a very large field behind the housing units. We would go out there to play and to watch the prairie dogs, which I thought were amazing. This was the only time my dad fought a transfer as he received orders to go to France. For reasons unknown, he bucked that order all the way to General Curtis LeMay who rescinded it. We returned to Westover in Massachusetts.

Chapter 12

HADLEY. Upon returning to Massachusetts, we rented an old farmhouse in Hadley, MA, for this new stint at Westover and the time was idyllic. It was on a dairy farm and I was allowed to visit our neighbors' barn, which I frequently did. I found being around the cows very reassuring. To this day the combined aroma of feed, hay and cow manure is comforting to me. Yes, I suppose that's odd to admit. Unlike other places I had lived, the kids in town were welcoming and living in a small town in the country was just fine with me.

Chapter 13

ANOTHER MOVE. In 1965, My dad came home with orders to go to Kadena AFB in Okinawa, Japan. I was excited to live in a foreign country – my first and only time doing so. We aimed west in our Ford van and headed for California to live with my grandmother until we could join dad. It was a wonderful trip. We headed south to drop our dog off with my other grandmother and then across the west and then north. We saw sunrise at the Painted Desert, marveled at the Petrified Forest and were in awe of the Grand Canyon.

Chapter 14

OKINAWA. The time spent there was two of the best years of my childhood. I loved the island, and its people. I joined a Boy Scout troop and camped and hiked all over the place. The military bases all had theaters and I was able to go to the movies a lot, which undoubtedly planted the seed that would bloom a few years later. I received my first allowance and was able to buy dreaded comic books, despite my mom's fears. Our parents drilled into us that we were guests on Okinawa and to treat everyone with deference and respect.

Okinawa. A family portrait from our stay in Okinawa. Left to right, the wretch, Dad, Mom, and Patrick.

Chapter 15

BOMB SCARE. Our scout troop did a 50-mile hike during Christmas break. We were camping in a park when a buddy of mine needed to urinate. He went into a grassy area, dug a little hole and discovered an unexploded Naval shell from WW II. The authorities were notified who came to remove it before it could cause harm. This was not uncommon on the island, which had been the site of the last greatest battles of the war. The remnants of the war were all around us. In our back yard at our on-base house was a Japanese bunker.

I loved the Boy Scout program I was in when we lived on Okinawa. It played significant role in my young life.

Chapter 16

ANOTHER MOVE. As you can see my father's job played a huge role in my childhood and now Dad was ordered to Vietnam. We came back to Massachusetts where my parents bought a house in Granby before my dad left for his new command at Bien Hoa air base outside of Saigon. It was a rushed, chaotic time fraught with the anxiety that Dad was in a war zone again, but for the first time during the lives of my brother and me. To say Granby was not a welcoming place is an understatement. This little New England town was tough.

Chapter 17

FARM LIFE IS FOR ME. Once my dad returned from Vietnam in 1968 and retired – three wars had been enough – he became a school teacher and we started a small farm that included a vegetable garden, fruit trees, chickens for eggs and meat as well as pigs. We had two Jersey cows I had to learn to milk, which were replaced by a herd of dairy goats, the nicest animals I knew. We rented land for hay production and my dad even tried to plow with a donkey, which confused me as we had two tractors. I appreciated my education.

Farm life is for me. Ah, New England, where fields are full of rocks! My mom and I digging a boulder out of a vegetable garden.

Chapter 18

INERTRON. In 1969, I was a budding film crazy kid. I wanted to learn everything I could about movies, especially horror, science fiction and fantasy. I discovered that people with my interests were publishing amateur magazines called "fanzines." This blew my mind. You didn't have to be an adult? A professional writer or artist? You could just do it? So, I started my own magazine in 1970. Luckily for me my dad had bought a spirit duplicator for printing stuff for his high school class, which meant I had my own printing press. My career as a writer had begun.

This very modest little fanzine meant a lot to the start of my interest in writing and movies.

Chapter 19

FREAK SHOW. High school for many people is difficult enough, but for me an extra layer of hell was added because my interests did not involve sports or cars, the two truly acceptable male endeavors in the Sixties and Seventies. I didn't drink or smoke dope, either. I was very appreciative of women but I was completely without confidence. Looking at old photos I could see why. I was the pimply-faced kid who liked monster movies, comics books, W.C Fields, Monty Python and the Marx Brothers. I published a fanzine and made Super 8 movies. I was a first-generation nerd.

Chapter 20

HIGH SCHOOL. While in high school, I not only launched my magazine, *"Inertron,"* but I became the editor of the school newspaper. It was clear to me that I wanted to have some sort of career in media. I loved listening to radio, as well as seeing every film I could. Television interested me as well but breaking into television seemed extremely unlikely. At the end of my senior year, I was told I needed to get an internship and did so at the Holyoke (MA) Transcript-Telegram, a daily newspaper. It was there I fell hopelessly and permanently in love.

Chapter 21

FIRST CONTROVERSEY. Foreshadowing much of my career, I had the first complaint about something I put in the high school newspaper I edited.

"The Granby High Thymes," (hey it was the early 1970s) included little bits I would write about movies. Sometimes it was reviews, sometimes I just made mention of a new release. My preview of *"Watermelon Man"* (about a white guy who wakes up black one day, starring Godfrey Cambridge) drew criticism from one parent that I shouldn't have written about an R-rated film in a high school publication. That R rating was going to corrupt some student.

My time as a high school newspaper editor won me "The Most Valuable Staffer Award" from the Transcript-Telegram. I'm seen here with Lorraine Browning, the newspaper advisor.

Chapter 22

THE TRANSCRIPT-TELEGRAM. In 1972, I wandered into the T-T offices for the first time. The newsroom was a large space with desks that each had a manual typewriter. There didn't seem to be assigned seats. You would sit and type your story on a roll of paper behind each typewriter. You would rip the story off the roll and hand it to the city editor who would edit it with a red pen. He would roll it up, put it in a plastic tube and put the tube in a pneumatic tube that carried it to the composition room upstairs.

Chapter 23

COMPOSTION. At the time, The Transcript was one of the last newspapers that was still using linotypes and hot lead to make the printing plates. The Linotype looked like a typewriter attached to a reservoir of molten lead overhead. The Linotype operators – short thin older men each with a cigarette hanging from their lips – would type up the story creating the lead type for the printing plate. I thought it was the coolest thing I had seen in years. Although I never got a byline for the stories they assigned for me, I knew that this experience was for me.

Chapter 24

CELEBRITIES. I continued my fanzine while attending the University of Massachusetts and realized the key to getting attention for an issue included getting a celebrity interview or two. Somehow, I was able to get the address of actor Buster Crabbe known for his role as Flash Gordon, among others. Crabbe was very accommodating and consented to a telephone interview. I was so nervous my leg was shaking the entire time I had him on the phone. The experience taught me the importance of doing research and trying to ask questions about topics that weren't obvious, such as his other roles.

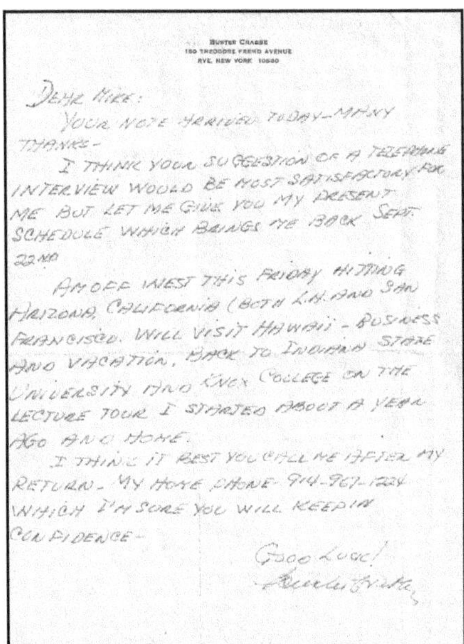

BUSTER CRABBE
150 THEODORE FREND AVENUE
RYE, NEW YORK 10580

DEAR MIKE:

YOUR NOTE ARRIVED TODAY—MANY THANKS—

I THINK YOUR SUGGESTION OF A TELEPHONE INTERVIEW WOULD BE MOST SATISFACTORY FOR ME BUT LET ME GIVE YOU MY PRESENT SCHEDULE WHICH BRINGS ME BACK SEPT. 22ND

AM OFF WEST THIS FRIDAY HITTING ARIZONA, CALIFORNIA (BOTH L.A. AND SAN FRANCISCO). WILL VISIT HAWAII - BUSINESS AND VACATION, BACK TO INDIANA STATE UNIVERSITY AND KNOX COLLEGE ON THE LECTURE TOUR I STARTED ABOUT A YEAR AGO AND HOME.

I THINK IT BEST YOU CALL ME AFTER MY RETURN - MY HOME PHONE 914-967-1224 WHICH I'M SURE YOU WILL KEEP IN CONFIDENCE—

GOOD LUCK!

Here is the letter I received from Buster Crabbe confirming the interview. I was thrilled.

Chapter 25

FREELANCING STARTS. I was told I should work at the campus newspaper at UMass, *The Daily Collegiate.* I went to the offices and didn't like the frat boy mentality I saw. So, I went to the local alternative newspaper, *The Valley Advocate,* and started freelancing for them. I was getting paid, which meant I started my professional career in 1975. The pay wasn't great by any means but it was a start. There was nothing quite like the feel of opening up a newspaper and seeing my byline. My assignments revolved around various popular culture subjects, which suited me fine.

PERFORMANCE

Divinely Outrageous

By G. Michael Dobbs

The woman on stage resembles a Kabuki Mae West on drugs as she propositions her audience, taunting them with offers of sexual favors.

They shout their approval at her obscene suggestions, and she responds, ". . . I'll be on my back until Christmas, but it will be the best time you'll ever have. . . . That reminds me of my next song, 'I'm Just So —-ing Beautiful.'"

With that cue, the soundman at the rear of the hall begins a pulsing hard rock beat, and Divine starts to sing.

"Outrageous" is the word frequently used to describe Divine, a 300-pound drag queen who built up a cult following in a string of semi-underground movies and now is attempting an assault on mainstream pop culture. Her performance at Pearl Street in Northampton last week was profane enough to melt Bibles at 100 paces.

Besides inviting members of the audiences to sample her sexual favors, she belched, snorted and sneezed in the microphone, used the mic and its stand as substitute phalluses, wiped her crotch with a kleenex and then tossed it out as a souvenir and revealed sexual details of the lives of the president and the first lady.

Divine's act is crude, even by the standards set by such entertainment figures as Tubby Boots and Buddy Hackett. The one-liners are not very witty, and the profanity has none of the rough charm of that used by Richard Pryor.

The joke is that everyone in the audience knows that Divine is really a man who dresses as a parody of a woman. The sexual twist makes her funny.

Divine came to prominence in the early '70s when Baltimore-based filmmaker John Waters starred her in his cult classic, *Pink*

Waters' earlier films, and featured "Smellovision" as its gimmick. Each member of the audience was handed a scratch-and-sniff card upon entering the theater. You just had to follow the cues in the movie to enjoy "Smellovision."

Divine's latest cinematic endeavor was in the critically roasted *Lust in the Dust.* Produced by *Polyester* co-star Tab Hunter and directed by Paul Bartel, *Lust in the Dust* was supposed to be a Western spoof with Divine vying for Hunter's affections against Laine Kazan. In the Valley, the film opened and closed in a week.

Amazingly, Divine does not refer on-stage to the films which built her audience. Rather, her act is a promotional tour to prime her fans for her stateside recording debut. Already signed with a British label, Divine has recorded an album and several singles. Her latest is a cover of Frankie Valli and the Four Seasons' "Walk Like a Man."

While some of her songs mock her image, many are conventional rock and roll. The impression is that Divine wishes to be taken fairly seriously as a singer.

After the hour long show, Divine signed autographs for her fans in a small dressing room backstage. Dressed in a red seersucker robe and without one of her trademark wigs, Divine looked almost fragile. Bald, with the exception of a ring of white hair, she/he was no longer fully in character. Instead of the loud obscene answers to questions Divine would have given, Glen Milstead greeted fans politely and efficiently.

A pair who had driven from New London told Divine that she had "made our night. . .our week." Another urged her to "do in the States what you did in Britain."

The fans were carefully watched by Bernard Jay, Divine's manager, and with good reason. One pair of fans, a man and woman both clad in leopard skin dresses, asked for

Divine: The sacred and the profane. (Tobey photo)

Time can have Madonna on its cover, why can't it have Divine?" he asked with a quiet laugh.

He credits his recording and club success in Europe to his manager, and claimed he was the victim of bad management earlier in his career. At no time does he mention John Waters.

Divine, he says, is a "cartoon," which he

been left alone."

Jay did remind him of the time performing in Queensland, Australia when local censors joined Divine onstage and told her what could and couldn't be said. And, there was also the time when an announcement of Divine's act caused a Salt Lake City nightclub to lose its liquor permit.

Since these incidents are relatively isolated,

Interviewing Divine was one of the freelance stories I did for The Valley Advocate.

Chapter 26

IN PERSON. My next celebrity interview was with the legendary publisher of *MAD magazine* (and the highly influential EC line of comics) William M. Gaines. I did this interview in person at the MAD offices in New York and I was in awe. Gaines had a custom-made bust of King Kong mounted in his window as if Kong was looking at him as he scaled the building. Several toy zeppelins were mounted from the ceiling and Gaines resembled a cross between Santa and Karl Marx. The visit and interview went very well and I talked to Gaines two more times.

William M. Gaines
485 Madison Avenue
New York, N. Y. 10022

NOV 7 1975

Dear Mike -
Sorry I couldn't see you - was in the midst of a crisis!
Lovely interview - very professional - I enjoyed it!
Thank you very much!
Bill Gaines

I received this note from William M. Gaines after I sent him the finished interview.

Chapter 27

GAINES ONCE MORE. I did a second meeting with Gaines after *The Valley Advocate* published the story. This time I wrote a piece for consideration in MAD, which I read religiously. I told Gaines that and he immediately summoned one of the editors, Nick Meglin, who brought me into his office and read the script. It was the longest five minutes of my life. Meglin was courteous but to the point. I had written in the style of another MAD writer and he said I needed to find my own voice, which was very good advice to a young writer.

Chapter 28

THOU SHALL NOT WASTE. I used the Gaines story in my fanzine as well as selling it to *The Valley Advocate*. This was a valuable lesson to me I learned early on. If you have a story that would fit in several different places, do so and increase the readership while hopefully making a little more money. I have used this principle a great deal to this very day. The Gaines piece was revised for a regional magazine called *"V Mag,"* and then I included it in my collection of celebrity interviews called *"15 Minutes with... 40 Years of Interviews."*

Chapter 29

THE HUBRIS OF YOUTH. As a movie guy I loved the Pleasant Street Theater in Northampton MA, an arthouse. It was there in 1975 I saw a compilation of Betty Boop cartoons and my mind was blown. I knew a little about the Fleischer studio, but I was very impressed by what I saw and there was little written about it. I decided I should research the studio and write a book. It was a very long journey that produced a wonderful friendship and many years later two books. *"Made of Pen and Ink: The Fleischer Studios"* is available online.

Max Fleischer and his animation studio have played a huge role in my life from college to today.

Chapter 30

AFTER COLLEGE. When I graduated in 1976, there were few journalism jobs in my area and it would be the better part of two years before I could find a gig at a newspaper. In the meantime, I worked as a stock man at a discount department store and then as a traveling developmental reading teacher working in several private schools. During the time at the department store, I kept freelancing. While traveling from school to school I did additional research for the Fleischer project. Still my goal was to land a reporter's job at a local newspaper back home.

Chapter 31

FREELANCING. I continued freelancing for *The Valley Advocate* for years and the publication allowed me to interview a bunch of interesting people that included spending time with the late film star Divine in her dressing room after a concert performance in Northampton, MA. She was very low-key and friendly. Also, for another assignment, I hung out backstage at a wrestling show with legendary grapplers Capt. Lou Albano, Pat Patterson, Pedro Morales, and Bob Backlund. Albano called pro wrestlers "the greatest professional athletes in the world." Who was I to argue with a man with rubber bands glued to his face?

My brother took this shot of the legendary wrestler Captain Lou Albano during my interview with him.

Chapter 32

LIFE CHANGES. After college my girlfriend and I broke up. One of her sisters was determined to fix me up with a classmate at college and threw a party for the introduction. Although a nice person, she didn't interest me as much as another woman attending, named Mary. It took me several months to screw up the courage to ask her out and much to my surprise she consented to a date in May of 1977. We married in 1978 and she has been supportive and patient of the challenging career I chose to pursue. Undoubtedly, I don't deserve her.

Chapter 33

FIRST GIG. I wanted to work as a reporter but there was a job open at *The Daily Hampshire Gazette* in Northampton, MA, as an ad salesman. I took that job figuring I could then transfer to the news department. Boy, was I wrong! One reporter came over to me and asked how did it feel to be a prostitute. I was too shocked to answer. I was a lousy salesman as I took 'No' as an answer. When I came back from vacation, someone was at my desk. He was my replacement, as I had been fired in absentia.

Chapter 34

WESTFIELD EVENING NEWS. I managed to land on my feet with a gig as the lifestyle page editor/writer for a small daily. This was my first full-time writing job and I enjoyed it greatly even though the pay was crap. It was also the only journalism job I did with my brother who remains a very talented photographer. The news department was small but had a lot of dedicated people who wanted to make a difference in Westfield, MA. Years later, proving the universe has a sense of humor, the company that owned my last paper bought the Westfield daily.

Chapter 35

BACK TO THE T-T. I left Westfield daily for a better paying job at the Transcript-Telegram, now using up to date technology. Again, I wrote and assembled a lifestyle page. The T-T was a place with a very dysfunctional management staff and the crap all flowed downhill. On Christmas Eve we all met at the Christmas tree and sang to the publisher. We then gave him a present. He did not return the favor – no party, no bonus, no time off. It was one of the most frustrating jobs I ever had. I was glad to be fired from there.

Chapter 36

HAVE A BACKUP PLAN. Based on my food stories for the T-T, I was able to secure a job as a line-cook at a seafood/steak restaurant. I learned a lot about that industry and found I enjoyed cooking. I kept on freelancing this time for the Amherst Record and for a very supportive editor who thought my work was just fine. The kitchen staff was a great group of people and the food itself was damn good, even if I did help cook it! The lesson learned is to accept a decent back-up gig while you regroup from a set-back.

Chapter 37

TALK RADIO. When I was at the T-T I wrote stories about WREB, the talk radio station in our market. I had listened to it while in high school and the format intrigued me. I had been a guest several times on the morning show talking about old movies and when that host left, I applied. I greatly enjoyed the job and stayed from 1982 to 1987. As the house liberal during the Reagan years, I received the best hate mail. While I did have fans, I also had people who listened every day just because they couldn't stand me.

Insight

'I like being a ham and I like being a journalist, talking about local issues,' says Michael Dobbs, above left, who has been dubbed the staff liberal. At top right is one of his on-air ... Chimelis.

WREB

500-watt station sometimes more than all

By DIANA L. TOMB
Transcript-Telegram staff

'It gives me the opportunity to talk to people you'd never in everyday life get the opportunity to meet,' says Jonathan Evans of his work at WREB.

The Transcript-Telegram did a feature story on WREB and the three hosts, me, Ron Chimelis and the late Jonathan Evans. I was described as "portly," but it was noted that I had a voice like a "well-worn sneaker, comfortable but not showy." I'll accept that.

Chapter 38

INTERVIEWS. What I loved about talk radio is that with a telephone you could have guests from around the country and people were eager to talk with you regardless of your market because they had something to sell: a TV show, a movie, a book, a belief. Generally, you received 15 minutes (sometimes a half-hour) for an interview from a publicist, so I learned to cut to the chase and try to ask the questions people really wanted me to ask. We received a great monthly newsletter filled with celebrities of varying degrees of fame who wanted to be interviewed.

At the Holyoke MA Irish Festival one year, I spoke with Gov. Michael Dukakis, who later was the Democratic candidate for president.

Chapter 39

WHO DID I TALK WITH? Okay you kids, don't know the following names? Then look them up: among many others Vincent Price, Lillian Gish, Keye Luke, Clayton Moore, Antonio Fargas, Anne Rice, "Weird" Al Yankovic, Emo Philips, Cassandra Peterson (Elvira Mistress of the Dark), Brian Grazer, George Romero, Alex Gordon, Fritz Feld, James Lydon, Massachusetts governor and presidential candidate Michael Dukakis, Sen. George McGovern, US Attorney General Elliot Richardson, Sidney Sheldon, Rick Moranis, Dave Thomas, Maureen O'Hara and a never-ending parade of local political officials and interesting people. Naturally most of the people to whom I spoke were local listeners.

Another out in the field interview with the famed Irish singing group The Clancy Brothers. I believe my brother also took this photo.

Chapter 40

COMMERCIALS. Part of being a talk show host was doing local commercial endorsements. Some businesses wanted a standard recorded commercial, while others wanted to have the hosts to recommend a business or product. I received an extra $1 for doing a live spot. I touted funeral homes, vacuum cleaners and car dealerships. My favorite was called "Cold Stick," a device you put in the freezer and then placed up your anus to treat hemorrhoids. Now imagine how I had to word this in the repressive 80s. They say every man has his price – mine was just one single American dollar.

One moment of my radio career that I will never forget is being the city of Holyoke's official Santa. Here I am with my nephew Andrew, who declared me to be "the real Santa."

Chapter 41

THE FREAKIEST MOMENT. I had interviewed legendary wrestling champ Bob Backlund once. It went okay. Months later, Backlund called me and wanted to be on my show. He had just lost his belt and did two hours with back-to-back calls. The day after I received a phone call from the owner of the WWF (now WWE), Vince McMahon. He said he knew I was a writer and wanted me to work for his new magazine. How did he know me? Was he listening to Backlund? I never took him up on his offer as it just seemed so freaking odd.

Chapter 42

SIDE HUSTLE. I worked a 40-hour week at the station and was paid a paltry $5 an hour. I needed a side gig, so I would turn the interviews I did into stories. I sold an interview with lawyer Alan Dershowitz to USA Today. I also took classes and got myself bartending jobs several nights a week to supplement my paycheck. There is nothing wrong with a part-time job as journalism jobs pay so little in too many markets. I liked bartending a lot but the liability bartenders carry was a little daunting so I left it when I could.

Chapter 43

LEAVING RADIO. I very reluctantly left radio (I really loved it) to become a program supervisor at a local historic house museum, Wistariahurst in Holyoke, MA. I love history and enjoyed working there doing a variety of things from helping to assemble exhibits, to running educational programs to doing publicity. The house was an old mansion and reputedly haunted, although I never heard or saw a thing. Perhaps my finest moment was putting together an art exhibit featuring the original work of the artists who created The Teenage Mutant Ninja Turtles as well as staging film presentations of classic movies.

I was quite proud of being able to develop this exhibit featuring the art of the folks who created the Teenage Mutant Ninja Turtles.

Chapter 44

SKIN OF MY TEETH. What I didn't know is the city that owned the museum was getting ready to slash its budget due to decreased revenues. Luckily for me I was offered a new job by the owners of an art house theater in Northampton, MA, so there was no employment gap. They were opening a new two-auditorium theater in nearby South Hadley. I had known them for years and I jumped at this opportunity to be part of the movie business. There are three branches to the industry: production, marketing/distribution and exhibition. I was happy to be in exhibition.

Chapter 45

TOWER THEATERS. I enjoyed the challenges of running an independent first-run theater and there were many. We had trouble getting first-run films the initial year that audiences wanted to see. The corporate-owned theater chains complained about our pricing to the studios. Things settled into a groove, though, and we started making money by running first-run commercial films. We also started showing *"The Rocky Horror Picture Show"* on weekends. That one film frequently made the payroll possible many weeks and although the clean-up after the shows with piles of rice, toilet paper and occasional vomit was challenging, it was worth it.

Chapter 46

COMICS. While at Tower, I did some freelancing public relations/marketing work at Tundra, the publishing company founded by Kevin Eastman, half of the team that created the Teenage Mutant Ninja Turtles. I assisted my friend Stephen Bissette with his book "Taboo," along with several others. It was a challenge because no one in the industry had yet determined where the marketing effort should be directed: at the consumer to create a demand or at the shop owner who was buying inventory. I tried both in an effort to get our books the place in the crowded 1980s market they deserved.

Chapter 47

MY MBA. Steve Bissette and I collaborated on a project for Tundra called "The Year in Fear," a calendar for horror fans. I learned a lot the hard way. It was designed not to be a functioning calendar – thanks art director. It came out too late (calendars are designed two years before sale). It didn't have a hole to hang on a display. It was too big for a counter. Tundra decided to dump it in Great Britain as a promotional item and had us autograph hundreds. Those copies were then relegated to a dumpster where we rescued a bunch.

Chapter 48

GUN TO MY HEAD. I truly enjoyed Tower Theaters, but the owners refused to offer any health insurance, which created a lot of stress. When a friend of mine recruited me for a job doing media relations at Western New England University at a much improved salary and a health plan, I reluctantly but sensibly resigned. While I made the right financial choice, I set myself up for seven years of pain. I had taught as an adjunct for many years there but being a staffer was a very different proposition. There was just one thing that saved my soul.

Chapter 49

ANIMATO. In 1992, a friend and I bought a magazine about animation for which I had been a contributor. It was called *"Animato."* The previous owner hadn't paid his printing bill and we obtained it for that fee. It was considered dead. I set up deals with distributors, contacted writers, introduced ourselves with publicists and were on the way with a quarterly schedule. Our advertisers included galleries, The Cartoon Network and companies that released anime. By day I was a lowly public relations guy, but any other time I was the editor and lead writer for a nationally distributed magazine.

I attended two of the home video trade shows to cover them for Animato! Here I am with Ren and Stimpy.

Chapter 50

ANIMATO PART TWO. The magazine gave me a chance to write a great deal about both classic and contemporary animation. The 1990s was the heyday of Nickelodeon, MTV and the Cartoon Network and I took advantage of it. I had the chance of interviewing John Kricfalusi and Bob Camp *"Ren & Stimpy"*; Joe Murray *"Rocko's Modern Life"*; Gabor Csupo and Arlene Klasky *"Rugrats"*; Craig Barlett *"Hey Arnold"*; Disney directors John Musker and Ron Clements; legendary director Ralph Bakshi; creator of Gumby, Art Clokey; Academy Award nominees Bill Plympton and John R. Dilworth; and animation gods Bill Hanna and Joe Barbera.

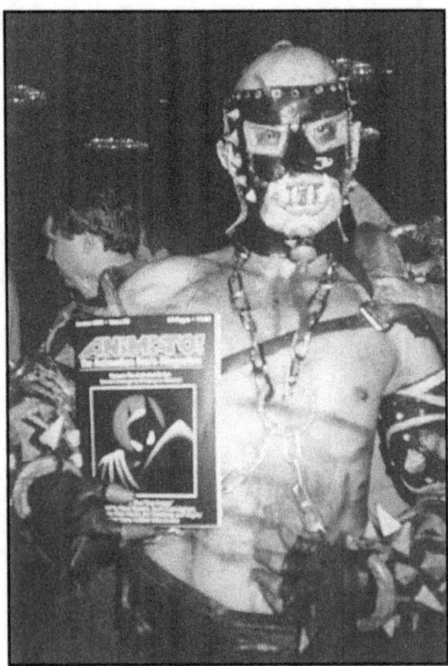

Promoting the magazine was a lot of work. Sometimes you have help, such as this unofficial endorsement of Animato by a member of the shock rock group GWAR at the Chiller Theatre show in New Jersey.

Chapter 51

ANIMATO PART THREE. One of my real pleasures was to interview voice actors. Historically the talented people who supplied voices seldom received screen credit for their performances that added so much to cartoons. The list included Jonathan Harris (yes, "Dr. Smith" from *"Lost in Space"*); Rob Paulson (*"Animaniacs"*); Maurice LaMarche (*"Pinky and the Brain"*); Billy West (*"Ren & Stimpy"*); Sid Raymond (*"Baby Huey"*); Don Messick ("Papa Smurf," "BooBoo Bear"); and Jackson Beck ("Bluto"). I also reprinted interviews I did with Mae Questel ("Betty Boop," "Olive Oyl"); and Jack Mercer ("Popeye," "Felix the Cat"). I even became friends with Jonathan Harris!

Actor Jonathan Harris befriended me and was a wonderful support of the magazine. I never had the guts to tell him as a child I regularly would pray that his character on *"Lost in Space,"* (Dr. Smith) would die so the Robinson family could get back to Earth!

Chapter 52

ALL GOOD THINGS END. In 1997, my partner decided he wanted out but I didn't have the money to buy him out of *"Animato,"* so he bought me out. Foolishly I allowed my ego to dictate my next move and I founded a new magazine called *"Animation Planet."* It ran two issues before the advertising bubble burst and distributors were being bought out by larger companies. As I filled out an application with a new distributor, whose terms would eat up any profits, I realized I may need to take out a second mortgage. I decided to pull the plug.

Chapter 53

LESSONS IN PUBLIC RELATIONS. I should have known my very first week what was in store for me at my new job at the college. A regular caller on WREB was Michael Meeropol, one of the two sons of Julius and Ethel Rosenberg. He was a professor of economics at the college. I loved talking to Michael as he was very bright and liberal. My boss told me that I was to have nothing to do with him as the college president wouldn't approve. So eventually Michael stopped asking me to get together for lunch. I think he knew why.

Chapter 54

LESSONS IN PUBLIC RELATIONS TWO. The local daily had a higher education reporter, a really good political reporter who had apparently been banished to this beat because of an alleged sin. I established a good relationship with him until the day the college president announced her retirement and said she wouldn't speak to the press. He wouldn't accept what I could give him, which was a one or two sentence statement. "You're either an idiot or a liar," he yelled at me over the phone. It took me many more months to rebuild the relationship. He never apologized to me.

Chapter 55

LESSONS IN PUBLIC RELATIONS THREE. I realized that people with PhDs in something other than communications didn't have a clue about effective marketing. All they knew is that they were very important and the world should know that. I have never encountered more ego and less common sense than my years working at a college. For them writing a textbook was front page news in The New York Times – so why wasn't I getting them the coverage they deserve? Because they didn't freaking deserve it! They didn't understand editors wanted stories about research and innovation to which audiences could relate.

Chapter 56

GOODBYE. I received several merit raises while at the college doing a job I hated for seven years. In the interview for a new position, I made the mistake of saying the professors weren't very media sophisticated. This bit of honesty eventually resulted in my termination as my boss was deeply offended. I thought she was a realist, but I was wrong. When she did fire me, the college paid me for the rest of my contract – an unexpected bonus. After my last day, my wife said I looked happier and healthier than I had for the previous seven years.

Chapter 57

BACK TO JOURNALISM. In 1999, I was very relieved not to deal with bullshit public relations problems any longer and gladly accepted a job at Reminder Publishing as the editor of one of its weekly papers, The Chicopee Herald. That was the start of a 22-year run, most of which I served as the executive editor, the most significant part of my career to this date. I was unusual as I continued working as a reporter as well as a supervisor. What that created was a perception from the readers that I, unlike my peers, was part of the community.

Chapter 58

PRINT IS NOT DEAD. Yeah, I know what you think, but we showed The Reminder's format of being a free weekly could draw back readers who were sick of daily papers cutting back on content. Decrease the number of stories and you create more reasons for readers to drop you. Newspaper owners have not understood this simple concept. They started a trend years ago of cutting content to boost profits. This has only led to an erosion of readership and advertising support. My publishers didn't care much for news coverage, so I just did stuff for readers behind their back.

Chapter 59

WONDERFUL PEOPLE. One of the pleasures of working at The Reminder were my colleagues over the years. I was blessed having some truly talented journalists as part of the team. I know I can't list them here as I'm sure I will leave someone out – a mistake of the brain, not the heart. I will note that members of the staff went on to work for their own media outlets as well as CBS News. Some left journalism because of the money, something that always makes me sad. Although there were a couple that caused problems, most were a joy.

Chapter 60

DEMOCRACY. Every news reporter, if doing the job well, plays a major part in sustaining our democratic way of life, which is indeed threatened. Without covering local government who would hold people responsible? I know every reporter wants to do big national or international stories. They are vital as well, but the local stories are those whose subjects affect people the quickest. Writing about snow removal efforts or how schools have improved or the activities of the police are vital to an understanding of how a community works. Reporters should be proud to know their efforts actually make a difference.

Chapter 61

TELEVISION. A few years back, I was approached by Focus Springfield, our cable access station, to host some programs. I was dubious. I am not a typical choice for TV. I'm old, overweight, white-haired and wear glasses. No commercial station would touch me. Yet, they saw something in me and I've had the privilege of doing a lot of interviewing on-air of local government officials and others. It's been a lot of fun and we have built an audience who watch our shows for content they are not getting from either the commercial stations or the local public TV outlet.

One of the programs I do for Focus Springfield is *"Government Matters,"* an interview show with various officials. Here I am (right) with Congressman Richard Neal.

Chapter 62

RETIREMENT. On Oct. 1, 2022, I retired from being executive editor and started freelancing for The Reminder. People have asked me why I still wanted to write for the paper. Isn't it time for the rocking chair? My answer is not one of ego, but of love of an activity. I enjoy reporting and if I can make a positive contribution to the newspaper I helped build, then why not? So far, the staff I once hired is still allowing me to be a small part of the organization. I'm very aware that status might change as all things do.

Here I am trying to say something profound at my retirement party. My brother Patrick took the photo.

Chapter 63

BOOKS. To date, I've completed seven books, all available on line: *"A Postcard History of Springfield;"* *"Escape! How Animation Broke into the Mainstream in the 1990s;"* *"Fifteen Minutes With: 40 Years of Interviews;"* my graphic novel under a pen name, *"Tales from the Runway: Dark Comedy from the Lives of Strippers;"* two volumes about the Fleischer animation studio titled *"Made of Pen and Ink;"* and the one you are holding. I have two more books in the works. One is about film fans turned producers Richard and Alex Gordon while the other is about cowboy star and actor Tom Tyler.

All of my books are available online, but this one is also in local Walgreens pharmacies. Whenever I see it, I make sure it has a prominent place on the rack.

Chapter 64

GEEZER. I see how many journalists are forced to work today and it breaks my heart. Some are told to post stories online without the benefit of an editor. Many are told they must take their own photos and video, while reporting. Everyone is trying to be the first to post a story, which can result in some faulty reporting. I don't blame the reporters; I blame the publishers and owners who demand we all compete in this stupid race. It's better to get the story correct than it is to get it first. Yes. I'm old school and proud.

Chapter 65

ROLE MODELS. There are several from the past who inspired me. Ambrose Bierce, reporter and short story writer defined "Reporter" in his *"Devil's Dictionary,"* as "A writer who guesses his way to the truth and dispels it with a tempest of words." Don Marquis was a wonderful columnist known for his satire. He once wrote "The chief obstacle to the progress of the human race is the human race." The third is the problematic H. L. Mencken who wrote, "Every normal man must be tempted, at times, to spit upon his hands, hoist the black flag, and begin slitting throats."

Chapter 66

WHAT THEY DIDN'T TEACH ME IN JOURNALISM SCHOOL BUT WHAT I LEARNED ON THE JOB

THE PRACTICAL ADVICE I RECEIVED. The late Professor Ralph Whitehead once advised his class that the most important interviews you will do will be in bars. He added that if a competitor drops his or her pencil at a press conference to kick it. And don't be afraid to use your elbows in getting first to a payphone to call in a story. Whitehead was a reporter in Chicago and clearly journalism is a blood sport in that town. I have never done any of this except for interviewing someone at a bar and those were not my important interviews.

Chapter 69

KNOW YOUR CIVICS. Who are the local elected officials you are covering? How does your local government work? Who is in the local delegation to the state capitol? If you've not reviewed local government and how it works, do so immediately. Know how a select board and a city council work and the differences between them. Understand the role of the town managers, administrators or mayors. Get all the names of all the officials with whom you work and do some research to understand context. Go to meetings before you have an assignment to get the lay of the land.

Chapter 70

AGENDAS ARE YOUR FRIENDS. Never, I repeat, never ever go into a city council, select board or school committee meeting without a definite reason to be there. Just turning up is not always worthy use of your time and effort. Always review a meeting agenda so you will know there is actually something newsworthy happening. This gives you the chance to research an issue so you can better understand the conversation in a meeting. Not all agendas are equal as some are very detailed, while others are just a bare outline. You need to learn the style of your municipality.

Chapter 71

GO WITH THE FLOW. If covering a public meeting you have to make the story work on its schedule not yours. A TV reporter once interrupted a public meeting I was at to say she needed to get some interviews to meet her deadline. The chair of the meeting coolly said he would be happy to do an interview once the meeting was over. The reporter sat back down and pouted. Your deadline is your issue, not anyone else's. Planning ahead and speaking to your editor to make sure you get what you need in a timely fashion is important.

Chapter 72

IN-PERSON OR REMOTE. A positive outcome of the pandemic was that many cities and towns started broadcasting meetings live and then storing them for future viewing usually through a public access TV station. This can mean you could be "in" two places at once as a reporter. The downside is being in-person is a great way to establish contacts and to ask follow-up questions after a meeting. Pick those meetings that being in-person would be a benefit to the story and watch the other meetings at home. You may want to review a recording in case there is any confusion.

Chapter 73

RELATIONSHIPS. Working as a reporter requires being flexible. Weekdays, week nights, holidays and weekends are all fair game for the job. I've had politicians call me at 8 a.m. on Saturdays to talk as well as late night. I actually had an assignment during our honeymoon. If you are with someone or married, you need a partner who understands such things and is willing to roll with it. It's not easy. Ask my wife. If you find such a person, I'd advise to hang onto them as best as you can. Make as much time for them as you can.

Chapter 74

COLLEAGUES. It's wise to treat your colleagues from other outlets respectfully. I have had solid friendships with "competitors" that resulted in getting help when I've missed something. But sometimes the competition needs a lesson. I had to get a photo at a press conference. A reporter from another outlet, who frequently would interrupt interviews, stepped in front of me, pulling his usual nonsense and I said, "If you don't move so I can take this photo I'm kicking you in the nuts." This was overheard by the mayor's minion. The other reporter moved and never did that to me again.

Chapter 75

EDITORS. Did anyone in school ever warn that you would encounter irrational, cruel and incompetent editors? Probably not. Consider this to be your warning. Just because they are management doesn't mean they know what they are doing. As an editor, I've tried to treat people far better than how I was treated. The worst kind of editor has a hidden agenda. One editor assigned me a story. He then re-wrote it so the subject was definitely defamed and kept my byline on it. It turned out he hated the guy and was using me. I was lucky I wasn't sued.

Chapter 76

EDITORS PART TWO. Another editor was a drunk who, when left in charge of the paper, always did something strange, such as having the headlines on the front page printed in orange for no reason. He also wrote about the city buying too much road salt not knowing the storage area he saw was owned by a company that sold road salt. His best story is when he came back from vacation, tossed a roll of film to the photographer and told him to make a contact sheet. The photos were of him and his wife at a nudist colony.

Chapter 77

EDITORS PART THREE. I had one editor who broke a cardinal rule and started dating one of his reporters. The reporter in question was seated near me and I got to watch her slide under her desk like a 13-year-old in order to talk with her boyfriend who was 20-feet away. He decided to make his girlfriend my boss and she wanted to get rid of me because she didn't like my writing. She waited months to fire me, torturing me along the way and terminated me in December before Christmas. I have never forgotten or forgiven either of them.

Chapter 78

EDITORS PART FOUR. The best editors I had were those who wanted to give you the context you needed to tackle a story and then let you have at it. Reporters need support and an editor willing to work with them. Micro-managing can lead to reporters seeking another job as well as harboring murderous intent towards their bosses. A micromanaging editor is showing a staff a real lack of confidence in their abilities. A good editor wants to build up a staff not tear it down. Editors need to question if they, not their reporters, are doing their jobs well.

Chapter 79

THEY ARE NOT YOUR FRIEND. It's important when you are covering a public official on a regular schedule to develop a working relationship with that person. A working relationship can be cordial and civil with the understanding that you may ask some hard questions – that's your job. It's not a friendship, though. Don't let yourself think you're pals with someone because you aren't. Don't go out to lunch with them (unless it's a working lunch) and don't drink with them. You have a job to do and they have a job to do so keep it civil, keep it shallow.

Chapter 80

PEOPLE ONLY TELL YOU WHAT THEY WANT YOU TO KNOW. This goes hand in hand with the previous chapter. Although you might find elected officials and others who actually tell you things out of some sense of doing the right thing, many of the people whom you encounter are only talking to you because the information they share furthers their goal. It's human nature for them to advance their agenda. It's your job to figure that out. Always listen with a very critical ear and always be ready to do your due diligence about information they chose to give you.

Chapter 81

BE SURE YOU MAKE CLEAR WHAT IS ON AND OFF AND RECORD. Elected officials play fast and loose with this concept and it's up to you to make the rules clear. If someone says, "I want to go off-record," when he or she concludes, ask them how the information could be re-phrased to be used on-record. And be sure to make clear when the conversation switches back to on-record. Without attribution, the veracity of any statement is on your shoulders as a reporter not on the person you interviewed. The person who is talking should be responsible for their statements.

Chapter 82

THEY LEAVE IT UP TO YOU. I had an experienced mayor, in an on-record conversation, tell me his city council was a "fucking bunch of old men" who needed a side income – pretty damning, yes? This was a real challenging call to make: quote him and he would never talk to me again or he would lie that he never said that. I strongly realized he was a bit of a weasel; I ignored his assertion. If I had printed a family friendly version of the comment, he would have just denied it and his supporters would have accepted it.

Chapter 83

PEOPLE WILL LIE. I did a story once about a couple who had just bought a bar/restaurant. They explained what they were going to do to improve it and called it a "dingey dive" before they took over. I used the quote and upon publication, the couple called me to say they had never said that. It seems the former owner saw the story and read them the riot act. They decided to put the blame on me. This is a great example of the need to record an interview if you believe there is any chance for some blowback.

Chapter 84

YOU KIDS TODAY. It used to be that when an elected official didn't want to answer a question, he or she (or their minion) would say something like "We have no comment at this time." Now, they simply "ghost" you if you ask your question they don't like in an email. A communications person for a local mayor did this to me and was actually proud when he admitted to me that he had "ghosted" me. I think he felt this new social protocol could be used to manage information and that he was being "cool." He was not cool.

Chapter 85

INTERVIEWING PART ONE: UNDERSTAND THE CONTRACT. When you have an interview with a newsmaker, celebrity, etc., there is a permanent unspoken contract. That contract basically sets out that you accept a newsmaker is talking to you because he or she wants to say something that will benefit them. In turn they understand you are speaking with them with your own questions in mind. So, ask them about their project, legislation, etc. and then make sure you ask the questions that will suit your story requirements. If they break the contract, you should feel free to break your side as well.

Chapter 86

INTERVIEWING PART TWO: DO YOUR RESEARCH. The talk show host Larry King reportedly liked to avoid doing research as he felt his professional ignorance would reflect the audience's lack of knowledge. He wanted his questions to be what his audience would ask. While I understand that approach – it served him well – I have always done my research and generally it has paid off in establishing a connection with the subject. An interview subject actually appreciates that you took the time to learn something about them and this will make the interview go smoother. Then it's easier to ask tougher questions.

Chapter 87

INTERVIEWING PART THREE: ICEBREAKERS. I've had opportunities to interview people whose work I admire. I sat down with actress Maureen O'Hara (look her up, kids). I've had a crush on her since I was 13. So, I told her that and I added I thought she was very underrated as an actress, She agreed with me and the interview went well. I did the same with Bill Cosby (before the scandal) and admitted I was a fan. He said, "Well that will make this easier" and it was easy. By the way, they can tell if you're lying to them.

Oct 16, 1986

Dear Mike -

Thanks for the tape. I enjoyed it very much and am glad to get it.

You do a splendid interview! Thanks again, and keep up your fine work. The program was incisive and most interesting for its film information and TV.

I have enclosed an autographed photo of myself for you. Hope you'll like it.

Again, thanks for the tape and if in the future you have reason to call on me, I am at your service.

Gratefully,

Keye 陸

When you get a note such as this one, you know you've done your job correctly. This letter is from the great Chinese American actor Keye Luke.

Chapter 88

INTERVIEWING PART FOUR: TRY NOT TO REPEAT QUESTIONS ALREADY ASKED. For instance, I had the chance to interview actor and director Leonard Nimoy. He had quit acting to pursue a serious love of photography and had a show of his work locally. I was questioned by a colleague why I didn't ask him about "Star Trek." I replied, "Because he has been repeatedly asked every question about Mr. Spock possible since the Sixties." Although sometimes you might be compelled to ask an often-repeated question, try to put a new spin on it if possible. Some celebrities will understand, some won't.

Chapter 89

INTERVIEWING PART FIVE: KNOW YOUR TIME. Generally, you will find that you'll be offered 15 minutes or so for a telephone interview with a celeb. While longer interviews are possible – and desirable – be aware that a quarter hour is more likely and can be enough for many stories such as advances. The key is to be prepared with questions and to use every second to get the information you need for a good story. I spoke with rocker Alice Cooper once. I had 10 minutes and I made sure I was ready. Alice, by the way, was a thorough professional.

Chapter 90

INTERVIEWING PART SIX: LISTEN. An "asshole buddy" of mine, who prided himself as a great interviewer, was writing a book about a famous comic book studio. He asked the same questions (he prepared a list) to every artist. He did not have a conversation with them. He did not actually listen to what they said and he did not do any follow-up. This is exactly not the way to conduct an interview. The best interviews are conversations with give and take and follow-ups. In his case the book was canceled and he had to refund the advance from the publisher.

Chapter 91

INTERVIEWING PART SEVEN: SOMETIMES THEY ARE ASSHOLES. I loved the work of singer songwriter Don McLean ("American Pie"). He was playing a local amusement park and I set up with his management time to do an interview. After his performance, he and his band went to ride the rides. He kept putting me off and finally I was angry enough to tell him if he didn't want an interview just let me know. He admitted he hated doing interviews and did speak with me but reluctantly. Don't be afraid to push back on someone who isn't treating you with respect.

Chapter 92

REVIEWS ARE FUN BUT MAKE THEM WORTHWHILE. The daily paper with which I competed liked to run reviews of shows that performed once in our town and then left. What is the point for a reader? They get to read how they missed a great performance? Sure, getting into a concert or event free is great for you, but advances are far better for a story. Tell your audience about an upcoming event and interview the performer. This is information that readers can actually use. Reviews of movies, TV shows and recorded music are fine and helpful to your audience.

Chapter 93

LOOK AT THE DAMN WEATHER FORECAST BUT DON'T TRUST IT. A good friend of mine, a great news photographer, told me he keeps several different coats in his car to be prepared for whatever weather occurs on the job. The last thing you need is to be standing unprotected in the rain covering something. Using an umbrella is unwieldy if you're taking notes. And please, wear a hat with rain or cold or sun. Protecting yourself is a lot more important than maintaining your "look," even if you're on television. Forecasters are frequently wrong, so be prepared like a scout.

Chapter 94

WEAR SENSIBLE SHOES. One spring day, I'm standing next to a TV weather forecaster at an outdoor press conference at a city park. She was tall, dressed in a blood red cocktail dress with stiletto heels. She was quite attractive, especially in the completely inappropriate party dress. I realize mid-way through the event that she was getting shorter and shorter. I glanced down and saw her shoes were sinking into the soft damp soil. Day to day you may not know where you will be so wear a pair of shoes that can keep you dry and warm. Screw fashion.

Chapter 95

FIGURE OUT YOUR OWN SYSTEM FOR TAKING NOTES. Everyone is different when it comes to taking notes. I prefer a traditional reporter's notebook and a pen. One woman I knew always took notes on a legal pad with a Sharpie. It was her system and it worked for her. I will always regret not taking shorthand in high school, as my mom suggested, but over the years I've developed my own system for notetaking. Today, many young reporters use audio recording on their phones. It doesn't matter what you do as long as you are able to have accurate notes.

Chapter 96

WHERE DO I GO ON ELECTION NIGHT. You will find yourself assigned to a race and you need to write a story about both candidates for that race. But where do you go first on election night, though? You have to be in two places at once, naturally. If you think who is going to be the winner, go to the loser's headquarters first. The loser's party will always break up sooner. You don't want to be standing in the middle of an empty hall. The winner will party into the night and you will have no trouble getting quotes.

Chapter 97

SOMEONE WANTS YOU TO EAT AT AN ASSIGNMENT. I was covering a congressional race and I was at the loser's party, waiting for him to concede. His wife had ordered a huge stack of pizzas for the crowds that hadn't come and urged me to eat. She was being gracious, but I politely declined. You don't want to be in someone's debt and eating can send a message that you favor one candidate over the other. And for your sake, do not take an alcoholic drink at an event, if offered. That sends an even more potent message of approval.

Chapter 98

PUBLIC RELATIONS PEOPLE CAN BE YOUR FRIEND. If you work with a public relations person who understands their job and understands your job, you will have an easier time getting the information you need and they will get coverage for their client. I'm pleased to say I've worked with many who have made my life easier. This does not have to be an adversarial relationship. The problem is too many of them are lazy and somehow feel answering a reporter's questions is interrupting their "busy" day, therefore causing some friction. Going over their heads to their boss is sometimes necessary.

Chapter 99

SELFIES. Looking back at my career, I realized I have very few photos of me with people I've interviewed. Back in the day, reporters simply did not do that. Today, with the pressure of social media, many young people feel the urge to get a selfie in many social and business situations. Please resist it as it can make you look unprofessional. I understand that you want to post proof that you just interviewed someone significant but please do not whip out your cell phone and pose. If you must, please do not flash hand signs or make a face.

Chapter 100

HAVE A GOOD TIME. If no one has told you that this job can actually be fun and rewarding, then please allow me. You will have some wonderful experiences, meeting interesting people and learning things every day. This is exactly why I've enjoyed the job over the years. Every day can be different. Every day gives you the opportunity to find out something you didn't know the day before. Depending upon your outlet and location, you may have some real adventures. Despite ineffective publishers and editors who have no clue how to be an editor, I've had a satisfying career.

To the Editor; 3-20-2001

Has anyone noticed as I have that some Bathroom tissue (toilet paper rolls) are less wider than they used to be? If the companies are going to make the paper tissue less wider than now, we are in big trouble. Oh well; back to the depression era when we used crumpled newspaper or leaves. What a way to recycle paper.

John J. Skok

I cannot conclude this book without including the best letter to the editor I every received. Mr. Skok, wherever you are, thank you for your insights.

Printed in the USA
CPSIA information can be obtained
at www.ICGtesting.com
LVHW010358150624
783213LV00014B/765